SUPERSTARS OF FILM

keanu reeves

York Membery

CHELSEA HOUSE PUBLISHERS
Philadelphia

Library of Congress Cataloging-in-Publication Data
Membery, York
    Keanu Reeves / by York Membery.
       p.   cm. — (Superstars of film)
    Filmography: p.
    Summary: Presents a biography of the actor best known for his
roles in the Bill & Ted movies and "Speed."
    ISBN 0-7910-4646-X (hc)
    1. Reeves, Keanu—Juvenile literature. 2. Motion picture actors
and actresses—United States--Biography—Juvenile literature.
    [1. Reeves, Keanu. 2. Actors and actresses.] I. Title.
II. Series.
    PN2287.R295M46 1997
    791.43'028'092—dc21
    [B]   97-16041
                                                  CIP
                                                  AC

ACKNOWLEDGMENTS
Aquarius
Ciby 2000/Recorded Picture Co (courtesy Kobal)
Sam Goldwyn/Renaissance Films/BBC (courtesy Kobal)
Hemdale (courtesy Kobal)
Nelson Entertainment/Orion (courtesy Kobal)
New Line (courtesy Kobal)
Orion (courtesy Kobal)
Polar Films (courtesy Kobal)
20th Century Fox (courtesy Kobal)

CONTENTS

Keanu and Barbara Hershey in Aunt Julia and the Scriptwriter

BEGINNINGS

Keanu Reeves was best known simply as the airhead star of the *Bill & Ted* films, until the box office smash *Speed* put him up there with the two Toms—Cruise and Hanks—in Hollywood's first division. Overnight his salary rocketed to $7 million a movie. It was a massive but not entirely welcome leap forward for the enigmatic new screen star of the nineties. With his exotic looks, unusual name, and love of Shakespeare, Keanu has always been different. A flippant remark he once made about really being nothing more than "bourgeois" couldn't have been further from the truth.

Born on September 2, 1964, in Beirut, Keanu's nomadic upbringing took him from Lebanon to Australia to New York before his family settled in Toronto, Canada. In the "Swinging Sixties," the era of "Flower Power" when change was in the air, parents everywhere were giving their off-spring all sorts of unusual names. Keanu's radical first name (pronounced "Key-aar-nu") reflects the Hawaiian origins of his father, Sam; it means "cool breeze over the mountains." At the time, Sam and Keanu's British mother, Patricia (who was known as Patric), were both students at the American University in Beirut. "My mother was just twenty-two when I was born," says Keanu understandingly. "She and my father were two crazy kids." But the good times were not to last. When Keanu was only four his father walked out, leaving Patricia with a young son and two daughters to bring up. The couple had grown apart and there had been fights about Sam's drug taking, which would be a source of embarrassment to Keanu himself many years later.

At his Toronto school Keanu was nicknamed "The Wall" for his defensive skills at ice hockey, but above all he is remembered as an insecure child, perhaps not surprising given his family's rootless past. He excelled neither at his studies nor at sports. "I even flunked gym," he said. On the plus side, though, his family did have money, thanks to a Canadian relative who had made a fortune from publishing and property.

The household where Keanu grew up was dominated by women, which helps account for his strong feminine streak. Patricia—a fierce, independent spirit—was unconventional, to say the least, wearing her hair in a peach-dyed buzz cut and amazing friends with her flamboyant style. She found work designing costumes for Dolly Parton and Alice Cooper, singers every bit as flamboyant as herself. Undoubtedly the bohemian Patricia first fired Keanu's enthusiasm for acting and the theater—pursuits he perhaps realized would offer him the best chance to forget about the past and look to the future.

Keanu began his acting career playing Mercutio in a Toronto production of *Romeo and Juliet*. "It was a community theater production I took part in when I was eighteen," he recalls. "That was how I got an agent." He went on to make a television commercial for Coca-Cola and, more significantly, landed a role in a Toronto television show, *Hanging In*. The show was short-lived but it gave him valuable exposure and was a showcase for his growing talents.

Several roles in modest Canadian feature films followed but it was his appearance in *Youngblood*, a low-budget 1986 film about an ice hockey romance, that first got him noticed. Aimed squarely at a teenage audience, one critic scathingly branded it "the kind of film you'd sooner forget." It starred

Rob Lowe as Dean Youngblood, a young hockey player who wants to try his luck as a pro and discovers that he has to be tough to handle the opposition's bullying tactics on the ice. Keanu played the team's goalie, so he spent most of the film hidden from view behind a protective mask. His name was eleventh in the opening credits, behind Patrick Swayze and just about everyone else in the cast. It was fifteen minutes into the film before he made the briefest of appearances, ambling though the changing rooms with a ticket receipt roll balanced on his head. And it was another ten minutes before he opened his mouth, to utter the less than immortal words "That man is an animal." But Keanu's moment of glory wasn't quite over—he got to say one more line and let out an ear-piercing scream. Thus his screen career was born.

River's Edge

HOLLYWOOD

For years many Canadian showbiz stars—William Shatner, Jim Carrey, and Pamela Anderson to name a few—have headed south of the border in a bid for fame and fortune. And Keanu Reeves was no exception, leaving his Toronto hometown for the bright lights of Los Angeles at the tender age of twenty-one.

It could have been a big mistake. The sprawling, smog-ridden city can seem a heartless, money-grabbing town where everyone dreams of Hollywood stardom and only the strong survive. Keanu, however, had already made some useful contacts thanks to his stage, television, and film appearances. Almost immediately he landed a role in *River's Edge*, a chilling story of how a group of teenagers respond to a senseless murder. In director Tim Hunter's small-town hell, the postpunk generation have neither morals nor feelings and don't care about much of anything. But Matt, the character played by Keanu, views things differently. Appalled by the murder, his conscience eventually gets the better of him and he goes to the police. Even though the film also starred Dennis Hopper, it was Keanu who stole the acting honors. "The film boasts the best cast of unknowns for years and Reeves, in particular, is superb as the moral center of the film," raved one critic. *River's Edge* opened Hollywood's eyes to the young actor's talent and set him on the road to stardom. But even though the 1986 movie was a bleak, disturbing look at delinquent youth, Keanu's character—like so many of the parts he has played since—had an inner purity. The actor himself recognizes this, stating, "I've always played innocents."

Keanu went on to have fun portraying a high school nerd in *The Night Before* (1988) and an off-beat free spirit sporting a truly bizarre haircut in *Prince of Pennsylvania* (1988). But his third film of the year, *Permanent Record*, confirmed his promise. At first the movie seemed to be like any other teen movie of the eighties, a rite-of-passage story about a bunch of high school kids coping with the pressures of adolescence. Our first glimpse of Keanu—who got star billing—shows him playing electric guitar in his bedroom. A friend bursts in and Keanu yells, "Hey, the party's tonight!" Dressed in T-shirt, torn jeans, and boots, his only worry in the world appears to be whether his first party is going to be a success. But suddenly *Permanent Record* changes tack. On the night of the party, the best friend of Keanu's character "falls" to his death from a cliff. Keanu is devastated, but when he discovers it was suicide his world caves in around him; he breaks up with his girlfriend and is suspended from school before finally coming to terms with the tragedy.

Critics raved about Keanu's performance. One said he was "excellent" (a word that would soon be permanently linked with the actor) and another praised the "sympathetic performance from the very happening Reeves." However, despite featuring music from former Clash star Joe Strummer, and a cameo from rock legend Lou Reed, the film itself got a mixed reception.

Ironically, it was about this time that Keanu himself had his only very real brush with death. Always something of a speed freak, his beloved British-built Norton motorbike careered off the road at 100 mph and into an embankment near his Los Angeles home. He ended up in the hospital with a ruptured spleen and two broken ribs, and he still bears a horrific eighteen-inch scar on his torso. It wasn't the only time Keanu's love of speed would land him in trouble. "I'm an awful rider," he admits. "Another time I got broadsided by a car and ended up doing a somersault and landing on the sidewalk on my back." However, the tragic death of a fellow movie star—and close friend—would soon mend Keanu's wild ways.

Reeves and Winter travel through time in
Bill & Ted's Excellent Adventure

PARTY ON, DUDE!

Thanks in no small part to Keanu Reeves and the very silly but very funny *Bill & Ted* films, Californian surf-speak has spread around the world. In *Bill & Ted's Excellent Adventure* (1989), air-guitar-playing Bill (Alex Winter) and Ted (Keanu) see themselves as two cool dudes; everything else is either "excellent" or "heinous." In their crazy world the Wild Stallyns, their fantasy rock band—neither can really play guitar, of course—will be "most triumphant." In the eyes of their teacher, though, they're hopeless, and in danger of flunking an end-of-year history presentation. Ted is threatened with an even more "heinous" fate—his dad wants to send him to a military school in Alaska to knock some sense into him.

But help is at hand in the form of Rufus (played by George Carlin), a figure from the future who travels back in time to help the boys pass their exams. Apparently, in the year 2688, the world worships a couple of party-loving dudes called Bill and Ted whose catch phrases—such as "be excellent to each other," "greetings, my excellent friends" and "party on, dude"—have passed into everyday language. With the help of a telephone kiosk (perhaps inspired by the British science-fiction television show *Dr Who*), the dim-witted duo go back to the past. Jumping in and out of different epochs, they collect historical figures ranging from

13

Beethoven to Billy the Kid, Socrates to Sigmund Freud, and confront them with West Coast culture. A hit with teenagers, *Bill & Ted's Excellent Adventure* soon gained cult status. And even many critics who generally frown on frothy, frivolous pictures found our heroes "endearing," a tribute to the inspired casting of Reeves and Winter in the lead roles.

With a bigger budget, the sequel did even better at the box office (and helped pave the way for the phenomenally successful *Wayne's World* films). *Bill & Ted's Bogus Journey* (1991) opens with the wicked De Nomolus (Joss Ackland) dispatching two look-alike androids back through time to present-day California, with the intention of killing the dudes. Our heroes gamble with death, meet the Grim Reaper—"How's it hanging, Death?" asks Ted—and beat him at board games like Battleship and Clue. They hang out in Hell—"Just like an Iron Maiden cover," they observe—visit Heaven, and then return to the present to "save the babes" and, of course, take part in the Battle of the Bands.

When *Bill & Ted's Bogus Journey* came out, the twenty-six-year-old Keanu said: "I could go on making these movies till I'm sixty." By then the critics, too, had got the joke and heaped praise on the "acutely observed, more cinematic sequel," raved about "the first-rate special effects," and talked about its dedicatedly dumb stars as "a comic pairing to rival Laurel and Hardy." As Ted would have said, they were most triumphant.

Keanu was so convincing as Ted, however, that some media types were soon implying he must be every bit as dumb as his character—that for all intents and purposes, he *was* Ted. "You are left wondering whether he's a philosopher or an airhead," sniffed one journalist. It's not hard to see how Keanu's "rambling inarticulacy," as one reporter put it, has prompted this interpretation. Perhaps recognizing the surf dude inside him, Keanu once joked, "When I'm dead I'll probably only be remembered for playing Ted!"

Androids Reeves and Winter in Bill & Ted's Bogus Journey

Keanu in Dangerous Liaisons

THE RISK TAKER

The fear of being branded a "real-life" Ted spurred Keanu on to take repeated chances with his career, some of which haven't paid off. In Ron Howard's *Parenthood* (1989)—the hit comedy-drama starring Steve Martin, Mary Steenburgen, and Rick Moranis—Keanu was typecast as the good-natured but none-too-bright son-in-law, Tod. Lawrence Kasdan's *I Love You to Death* gave Keanu the opportunity to reveal more of his obvious gift for comedy in his portrayal of a virtually brain-dead would-be assassin.

But Keanu's pre-*Speed* career saw him consciously putting distance between himself and the rest of the eighties Hollywood Brat Pack—with whom he'd never had a lot in common anyway—by appearing in big-screen costume dramas and Shakespearean adaptations as well as arthouse films, none of which had obvious appeal to his young audience. His first stab at costume drama was Stephen Frears's *Dangerous Liaisons* (1988), starring Glenn Close, John Malkovich, and Michelle Pfeiffer. Set in pre-Revolutionary France, it's a story of power, cruelty, and deceit. The monstrous Marquise de Merteuil (Close) and Vicomte de Valmont (Malkovich) spend their days planning seduction and revenge. And in a role light-years away from Ted or any of his other high-school-drop-out characters, Keanu bravely tackled the role of Chevalier Danceny, an idealistic young man corrupted by the Marquise.

The 1990 film *Aunt Julia and the Scriptwriter* (also known as *Tune in Tomorrow*)—based on Mario Vargas Llosa's acclaimed novel—also challenged the accepted view of Keanu as a star of contemporary youth films. Set in 1951 New Orleans, it starred Barbara Hershey as Aunt Julia, an attractive thirty-six-year-old divorcée who is searching for a new husband but instead falls for her twenty-one-year-old nephew-by-marriage, Martin (Keanu), a news writer at the local radio station. The arthouse comedy romance, which also featured *Columbo* star Peter Falk, got mixed reviews; it was called everything from "a thoroughly enjoyable romp" to "a hit and miss affair." And while it was something of a shock to see Keanu in a bow tie (it was probably the first time he'd ever worn one), his short, slicked-back hairstyle showed off his chiseled good looks to perfection. Not for the first time, though, many critics were unimpressed. One thought he "seemed to be struggling" in the part, while another found his "forced southern accent distracting."

In its own way, 1991's *Point Break* was just as big a challenge—it was Keanu's first straight "action" film. And if it weren't for *Point Break*, he would never have landed the *Speed* lead role. *Point Break*, a high-octane buddy-buddy cop thriller, was set among California's surfers and sought to capitalize on the twenty-six-year-old actor's growing heart-throb appeal. He played an FBI agent with the unlikely name of Johnny Utah, who goes under cover to crack a gang of bank robbers decked out in masks of former U.S. presidents. Keanu shared top billing with Patrick Swayze, with whom he'd worked in *Youngblood*. Both their careers had since prospered, and though they didn't become buddies, they did get along well together.

Once again Keanu's hair was short (although not as closely cropped as it was to be in *Speed*), and judging from his bulging biceps, he'd been pumping iron. The dopey teen character was now replaced by a tough, athletic young man who leaps through windows, packs a mean punch, and even

jumps out of a plane without a parachute. It was a performance that pushed all the right buttons with viewers.

In contrast, neither *Bram Stoker's Dracula* (1991) nor
Much Ado About Nothing (1993) enhanced his reputation as
an actor. But just as importantly, neither affected his
box-office bankability. Francis Ford Coppola's operatic
version of the horror classic certainly did good business at
the box office but it was less well received by critics.
Flamboyant British actor Gary Oldman, as Dracula, headed
an all-star cast that included Keanu (as English lawyer
Jonathan Harker), the always marvelous Anthony Hopkins,
and the bewitching Winona Ryder. But Keanu was singled
out for attack by the press: "His casting can't be described
as inspired—the poor boy can't cope with acting and
sustaining a British accent." Even the Hollywood magazine
Premiere sniped, "He's less than persuasive—his Valley boy
persona simply dons a stuffed shirt." Unusually for an
actor, Keanu now seems to agree. "My performance was
too introverted, closed-in, and safe," he admits. "In hind-
sight, I should have taken more risks. Francis tried to spur
me on to greater heights but I just couldn't reach them.
I didn't act very well."

His role as Don John, villainous brother to Denzel
Washington's prince in Kenneth Branagh's version of *Much
Ado About Nothing* also attracted criticism, though the film
was generally well received. One critic called Keanu "two-
dimensional" in the role and another scoffed at his "balsa
wood performance." But at least he had the courage to
tackle the part, and the good grace to wave his usual star fee,
agreeing to share a villa in Tuscany where the film was being
shot and even to cook his own food.

Perhaps the biggest risk Keanu has taken in his
career, though, was appearing in *My Own Private Idaho*, a
controversial adult "road movie" about a pair of low-lifes. A
lonesome young hustler, Mike (River Phoenix), and a hand-
some mayor's son, Scott (Keanu), take to the road in search

of Mike's long-lost mother, rubbing shoulders with a Shakespeare-talking bum along the way. Despite its strong language, explicit scenes, and documentary-style footage of real-life hustlers, the film is stylish, occasionally funny, and often moving.

Defending the film, an emotional Keanu says, "I'm surprised people are indignant, unless it's at the despair in the world the film examines." Undeniably a bizarre vehicle for both the young actors, *My Own Private Idaho* proved something of a notorious picture as well as being a critical success. Critics raved over River's performance but Keanu—who was back to his usual scruffy self in the film—took his role very seriously and received generally good notices. "If Reeves was overshadowed by Phoenix," said one reviewer, "this was more the role as written than played."

By the time Bernardo Bertolucci cast him as Prince Siddhartha in 1994's arthouse epic *Little Buddha*, Keanu was "a million dollar man on the make," according to one movie magazine, but he was yet to appear in a megabuck box-office hit. The ambitious $40 million film, also starring Bridget Fonda, tells the tale of the sixth-century Indian prince who became Buddha. Again Keanu faced something of a challenge but his "conversion" to Buddhism—which he credits with transforming him from teenage dude to serious actor—helped him come to grips with the role: "It's really altered my perception of life. I'd never really meditated before. Nowadays I'm a more sensitive person."

During filming, Keanu was struck down with food poisoning and laid low with fever, but the locals showed little sympathy. "They say it's because us Westerners have weak stomachs," he recalls. Keanu was also amazed to discover that he was something of a heartthrob even in Bhutan—which has no television and only one movie theater—and wherever he went, Nepali girls would beg him for his autograph.

Largely shot at a monastery in eastern Bhutan, *Little*

Buddha was as memorable for a bronzed Keanu in flowing robes and jewelry as for Bertolucci's trademark lavish sets and scenes. But the reviews were very mixed; at least one critic was unable to resist a dig at Keanu: "He still has an air of Bill and Ted around the edges."

Would he never be able to put the air-guitar-playing bozo behind him? Ironically, his next film would lay Ted's ghost to rest for good.

Keanu and Sandra Bullock in Speed

SUPERSTAR

The "bomb on a bus" blockbuster *Speed* was the film that made Keanu Reeves a superstar. Released in June 1994, it knocked Arnold Schwarzenegger's *True Lies* off the top spot and went on to gross $120 million. It was equally successful in other countries, and has become one of the most popular video rentals ever. It was a phenomenon—but a phenomenon that nearly didn't happen.

The film was Dutchman Jan De Bont's first as director. He'd already worked as a cinematographer on action movies like *Die Hard* and *Lethal Weapon 3*, but saw *Speed* as an opportunity to bring a fresh approach to a well-worn genre. "I had worked with Bruce Willis, Mel Gibson, and Sly Stallone," he says. "And I was desperate to find a new face because I felt like we'd seen all those other actors for so long." De Bont wanted his action hero to be tough but vulnerable, a sensitive strong guy, not a macho control freak. After seeing Keanu in *Point Break*, De Bont thought he was perfect for the role.

However, there were obstacles to be overcome. First was Keanu's own reluctance to make an action film. He disliked *True Lies* so much that he walked out of the film and is on record as saying that he has no ambition to be the new Schwarzenegger or Stallone. "When I was first approached to be in *Speed* I had a lot of doubts," he says. "It was wonderfully over the top but the story was cliched, the dialogue was bad, and the hero cracked jokes that were almost perverse. But I knew it could be a great film if the script problems were ironed out and it had a director with vision."

The second obstacle to overcome was the attitude of the film studio, Fox, toward Keanu. Unconvinced of his action-movie credentials, it insisted on pairing him with a big-name actress—something De Bont resolutely opposed. "I told them I wanted someone believable," he says. "Not a beautiful face, but a strong feisty woman." He chose the little-known Sandra Bullock, who'd starred opposite Stallone in *Demolition Man*. "Fox didn't go with it for a long time and only finally agreed two weeks before shooting on the film began. It was a nightmare—but I knew Keanu and Sandra would be a great combination."

In *Speed* Keanu plays SWAT policeman Jack Traven, who finds himself up against a master blackmailer and explosives expert (Dennis Hopper) who has planted a bomb on a city bus that is set to explode if the vehicle's speed drops under 50 mph. That's when Keanu springs into action—and claims his action crown. Three months in the gym helped him put on some muscle, and he arrived on the *Speed* set with chiseled shoulders and a bull neck—looking like a man who could handle himself, but not as muscle-bound as some other action stars.

De Bont also insisted that Keanu's hair should be cropped for the part. "The thing with Keanu is that he looks very boyish and I wanted him to look like an adult," says the director. Keanu was duly dispatched to the barber's but got a little carried away. "I had what they call a one-cut," says the actor. "Some people thought it was too extreme because they could see my scalp." Studio bosses went crazy. Says De Bont, "They asked me, 'Who told him to cut his hair? We have to get him a wig—now!' I said, 'No way are we going to get him a wig.' They called Keanu's manager and agent and wanted to postpone the film. I said, 'No way, we start in two

Reeves did many of his own stunts in Speed

weeks.'" Of course, that haircut would generate almost as much press coverage as the film itself. Women everywhere went wild over the actor's new look, and men flocked to their barbers asking for a "Keanu."

To help draw his star into the film, De Bont encouraged Keanu to do as many of the stunts as possible. So despite being banned from playing contact sports during filming in case he got injured, the guy seen clinging desperately to the roof of that bus was the cinema's latest action hero—doing it for real. The speed-loving star literally took his life into his hands during the making of the movie. In one scene, he took a breathtaking leap on to a runaway bus; in another he slid under the bus on a makeshift trolley. "There were no safety wires," says director De Bont. "One slip and it would have all been over, not just for Keanu but for all of us as far as the film was concerned. The stuntmen who were standing by couldn't believe he wanted to do these things." The actor did 90 percent of the stunts himself, according to De Bont, but Keanu has no doubt that driving the Jaguar on a freeway was the most fun. He recalls, "The stunt co-ordinator would say, 'You're going to go through this car and this car, and I'd be surrounded by stunt drivers and he'd say, 'Don't worry, you can't hit these guys, even if you try, now go for it.' Man, it was a blast."

Midway through filming, though, came the bombshell that his close friend River Phoenix had died from a drug overdose outside actor Johnny Depp's trendy Viper Club. Phoenix, who was just twenty-three, had described Keanu as being "like an older brother." And Keanu was hit so hard by the news that he reportedly locked himself away for a week. "It scared the hell out of him," says De Bont, who changed the shooting schedule to work around Keanu. "He became very quiet and it took him a while to work it out. I think it put an end to his wild period."

Reluctant to discuss the subject, Keanu comments, "All I can say is that I have never felt a thing like this before in my life. It was very sad, and something beyond sad. I don't know what it is, just that you sob for hours." However, his conversion to Buddhism helped him come to terms with the tragedy, and he believes River will come back in another life. "I don't know where he is now but I believe in reincarnation," he says.

His costar, Sandra Bullock, was also hit by the traumatic breakup of her four-year romance with actor Tate Donovan, who was convinced she had cheated on him with Keanu. "The breakdown of my relationship has been the most shattering experience of my life," she said at the time. "It's a case of him getting the wrong end of the stick because I only ever kissed Keanu in front of the film crew. I know just about every girl has a crush on him—and he's a terrific guy, kind, respectful, and good-looking on the inside too—but we're just friends."

Speed was a hit with both the public and the critics, who called it "brilliant," declared it "the perfect action film," and praised Keanu's "divine presence." *Premiere* commented that his performance had "inflamed the box office and put him on Hollywood's most wanted list." But in interviews, Keanu was eager to share the glory with the rest of the cast and crew: "For me it was very much an ensemble piece, not a star turn. It's Jan's film. He improved the script and Fox put extra money into the special effects."

Suddenly, everywhere you looked—magazine covers, newspapers, billboards—the film's clean-cut, steely-eyed star stared back. A teen pinup for a long time, Keanu Reeves was now indisputably a sex symbol to rival Tom Cruise, Mel Gibson, or Richard Gere. He was dubbed the "sexiest man in America" and voted "the world's most kissable star." It was flattering and could easily have gone to Keanu's head, but when asked about his sex-symbol status, he typically laughed it off, saying, "It's ridiculous."

As luck would have it, though, just weeks after *Speed* shot Keanu to worldwide fame, the past—in the shape of his father, Sam—cast an ugly shadow over his life. The fifty-two-year-old drifter, whom Keanu had been helping financially for years, was jailed in his native Hawaii for ten years for supplying cocaine and heroin.

The actor refused to comment about his father but a cousin, Leslie, said, "He's very angry. It's the last thing he needs. He feels nothing but contempt for Sam and has vowed never to help him again." Horrified studio bosses feared the adverse publicity would jeopardize the film's success, but they needn't have worried. Besides, how could Keanu be held in any way responsible for the actions of a father who'd walked out on him when he was four?

With the world at his feet, Hollywood insiders expected Keanu—who could now command a fee six times his pre-*Speed* salary—to start work on another blockbuster to consolidate his new star status. But it was the last thing on his mind.

Dennis Hopper played the master blackmailer in Speed

With Kenneth Branagh and company in Much Ado About Nothing

TO BE OR NOT TO BE

After *Speed* hit the jackpot, Keanu turned down a whopping $11 million to star in *Without Remorse* (a big-budget adaptation of Tom Clancy's best-selling novel) and rejected the chance to play a hit man alongside Robert De Niro and Al Pacino in *Heat*, all for the lead role in a small Canadian production of *Hamlet*.

Just about everyone in cash-crazy Hollywood expressed surprise at the decision, especially when they learned he was being paid just $2,000 a week to tread the boards. But they missed the point—making money had never been Keanu's prime motivation in life. Anyone could see that from the films he'd made; he was more interested in extending his range as an actor.

"I had the opportunity to play the part and couldn't turn it down because I've loved Shakespeare ever since reading *Hamlet* at school," he said during rehearsals. "The first thing that drew me to *Hamlet* was his angst. It's very audacious for me to take it on—I haven't played any of the larger Shakespearean parts—and a bit daunting."

However, his decision was certainly good news for the city of Winnipeg, not the sort of place many people usually visit in the winter, when the temperature plunges to a bone-chilling minus 20 degrees. And all of the 22,000 seats for the twenty-nine-day run at the 800-seat Manitoba Theatre sold out in advance, despite costing as much as $150 each.

In an attempt to stop the production from turning into a circus, Keanu asked to be treated as just another actor. But despite doing his best to keep a low profile, driving around in a battered Volvo and refusing to take curtain calls alone, this request was hopeless. The moment his plane touched down, the prairie city was gripped by Keanu fever—after all, it wasn't every day that one of Hollywood's hottest stars came to town. Fans flocked to snow-bound Winnipeg from as far away as Japan, France, and Finland, many without tickets. And seats that normally sold for about $50 were soon fetching more than $1000. The honor of being Keanu's number one fan went to Wendy Carey, aged forty-three, who flew in from Melbourne, Australia, to spend a month in Winnipeg, seeing *Hamlet* twice a week for four weeks.

Typically, Keanu only had to pay one visit to the normally quiet Pocket Bar and Grill and for weeks afterward it was packed with adoring fans. And he nearly caused a riot at a local shopping mall when he left his credit card in a clothing store. Foolishly the manager paged him on the public address system, and the store was swamped in seconds. "It was a zoo," said a shop assistant. "You couldn't move for women of all shapes and sizes."

Businesses were quick to cash in on Keanu's popularity, and soon had a flourishing trade in T-shirts and baseball caps carrying Hamlet quotations. The local paper, the *Winnipeg Free Press*, launched a "Spot Keanu Reeves" hotline but was forced to scrap it after being flooded with calls from fans desperate to see the star in the flesh.

Opening night in January 1995 finally came and everyone from the province's governor-general to Winnipeg's female mayor were in attendance, as was a ravenous pack of bloodthirsty critics. Strangely though, many of Hollywood's big shots, suspicious of the entire affair, simply pretended it wasn't happening. It was to be their loss. Although one critic wrote, "It turned out to be Keanu's not wholly excellent adventure, he was nervous, gabbled his lines like a learner driver and looked like the lead actor in a school play," most agreed that although he started nervously, Keanu quickly grew into the role, "projecting himself as an agile, animal Hamlet with bags of swash and buckle." One of the most glowing reviews appeared in the prestigious London *Sunday Times,* whose correspondent raved, "He's one of the top three Hamlets I've seen, for a simple reason: he is Hamlet. He is solitary and resourceful, won't submit, and like Hamlet, has a world within himself."

But perhaps the most heartwarming response came not from any of the big-city critics who descended on Winnipeg en masse—many in the hope of seeing Keanu slip up—but from a local high school teacher, Kenneth Clark, who summed up the situation when he said, "He has rekindled interest in the world's greatest playwright for a whole generation. He has made Shakespeare come alive for my kids and almost everyone else under fifty." That alone was an achievement of which Keanu could be proud.

Reeves and River Phoenix in My Own Private Idaho

IN THE PUBLIC EYE

Following the worldwide success of *Speed*, the actor's private life came under closer scrutiny than ever before. Despite his easygoing manner, Keanu had always managed to keep this part of his life pretty much hidden from public view. But now that he was such hot property, everyone wanted a piece of him, from vendors selling bootleg Keanu merchandise to ruthless tabloid editors.

Surprisingly for someone so rich—by now he is worth millions—Keanu leads a bohemian existence, in some ways echoing his rootless childhood years. Unlike most Hollywood stars, who snap up palatial homes overlooking the Pacific and start living the high life as soon as they're in the money, the lanky, six-foot-tall Keanu lives in Hollywood's famous Château Marmont Hotel. Apart from his bike, hockey stick, guitar, and a mountain of clothes, he owns little.

"I don't need a house," he says. "I prefer to be free, unfettered. I like being in the desert or high in a tree. I'm not a homebody type of guy." He's never really hung out with the "in" crowd in L.A. Why not? "I don't have enough of a personality," he jokes, adding, "I lead a very simple life." He's often seen speeding to his agent's Beverly Hills office on his 1970 Norton motorbike to pick up some new scripts, then stopping at Little Frida's, a West Hollywood coffee shop, where he'll read them while sipping cranberry juice.

He did join a roller hockey team, the Hollywood Hoofs. But the most important thing in his life outside the movies is his "folk thrash" band, Dogstar, and his best friends are essentially the other members of the band. He often gets together with them in the early evening for a meal at one of his favorite restaurants—either Café des Artistes, a funky bistro, or Quality Foods, a Generation X hangout—before going on to play at a club.

The four-piece band, for whom Keanu plays bass, started out as a fun hobby but there is talk of them landing a six-figure record deal. They opened for superstar rockers Bon Jovi at one L.A. gig, and showbiz pals like Danny De Vito, Tom Hanks, Sandra Bullock, and Rosanna Arquette have caught Dogstar in action. They have even embarked on a twenty-five-date U.S. tour and visited Japan. Described as "an updated Clash," the members of Dogstar write their own material but also play cover versions of songs like The Jam's "Modern World." "It's just a chance to have some fun and free beer with friends," says Keanu modestly. "Seriously, though, I do it for kicks but I want our music to be good. If people pay, I want it to be worth their time." A friend adds, "He doesn't see why the two careers—movies and music—can't run hand in hand."

In between, Keanu goes back to the Château Marmont, where he will meditate, or heads out to the home of his elder sister, Kim, in the L.A. suburbs for a few days. She is probably closer to him than anyone else—and he has lavished gifts on her, including a horse. "He looks on her as a mother, sister, and friend," says a family friend. In the evening they will watch a video, or she will cook him dinner and they will chat over a bottle of vintage Bordeaux wine.

He was devastated when he learned that she had developed lymph cancer, and he vowed to support her during the grueling five-year treatment. "At one point Keanu thought she was going to lose her battle with the illness and he used to break down in tears," says the friend. Kim lost all her hair after chemotherapy but then doctors told her the cancer was in remission. To celebrate, Keanu took her to the Oscars, the hottest date in Hollywood's calendar.

Over the years Keanu has been linked with a number of beautiful women. He reportedly had a fling with songstress Paula Abdul and was spotted with *Baywatch* star Pamela Anderson. He was also once seen with *Basic Instinct* star Sharon Stone in the Château Marmont's outdoor pool. He's never been short of female admirers, but he never seems to have enjoyed a serious, ongoing, relationship. "I've had a few relationships but . . . they haven't lasted."

In the gossip-driven, hysterical world of the movie business, the absence of a woman in his life fueled reports by the Hollywood rumor machine that Keanu was bisexual. Speculation had begun in 1991 when, during an interview to publicize *My Own Private Idaho,* he was asked if he was gay. Keanu denied it yet added, "But ya never know!" Since then it has emerged that the late River Phoenix had a crush on Keanu during the filming of *My Own Private Idaho*, and that a gay activist group had named a dance, the "Keanu," after him.

Then in the summer of 1995 came the rumor to end all rumors. A French magazine, *Voici*, sensationally claimed that Keanu had married gay record mogul David Geffen at a bizarre secret ceremony on a beach in Mexico. Newspapers and magazines throughout the world carried the allegation, which studio bosses feared would be the kiss of death for Keanu's box-office appeal.

"I've never met the man," laughed Keanu in an interview with *Vanity Fair* magazine. "It's so ridiculous I find it funny. It's a joke. Somebody took the magazine for a lot of money. I'm sorry, they've got the wrong guy." His mother, Patricia, declared, "It's the craziest thing I've ever heard." Geffen, who also strenuously denies the story, says, "It's just an ugly, mean-spirited rumor meant to hurt him because he's a movie star." Yet Keanu refused to categorically deny all rumors that he was homosexual, saying, "There's nothing wrong with being gay, so to deny it is to make a judgment. And why make a big deal of it? If someone doesn't want to hire me because they think I'm gay, I guess I'll have to deal with it. But otherwise it's just gossip, isn't it?"

Sky-diving encounter with Patrick Swayze in Point Blank

"Worst kiss of the year"? from A Walk in the Clouds

WIN SOME, LOSE SOME

Most actors would have been content to put their feet up after *Speed* and enjoy a well-deserved rest, but not Keanu Reeves. In keeping with his new policy of following a big-budget film with an arthouse flick, he appeared in *Even Cowgirls Get the Blues*, in a cameo role as a nervous artist. On paper the film must have sounded promising, and the 1976 book on which it was based had gained a cult following. The movie boasted a splendid cast that included Uma Thurman and John Hurt, as well as a soundtrack by songstress kd lang. However, by the time it reached the big screen, the story seemed extremely dated. Most of the gags didn't work on film; it was panned in the press and died at the box office.

The film industry had much higher hopes for Keanu's next movie, *Johnny Mnemonic*, a *Blade Runner*–style futuristic thriller adapted from William Gibson's cult cyberpunk novel and also starring tough-guy actor Dolph Lundgren and rapper Ice-T. Set in 2021 in a world ruled by multinational companies, Keanu was cast as a bio-enhanced data courier whose brain is loaded with the world's most valuable information—the formula for a cure to a "future shock" disease.

So confident were the TriStar studio bosses that they brought forward the release date of the film to May 1995. But their hopes were to be dashed. Critics swiftly dubbed it

41

Johnny Moronic, and following the bad reviews it just couldn't compete head-to-head against the summer's two big movies, *Batman Forever* and *Apollo 13*. Directed by Robert Longo, the picture was lucky to recoup its costs. "It's not the vision that William, Robert, and I had," an agitated Keanu later said. "It's been recut and isn't the film we shot. For three months I was playing a guy who didn't want his memory back, and six months later I do a scene where I say, "I want it all back." It's a very different movie."

His next film, the $20 million *A Walk in the Clouds*, was Keanu's first real outing as a romantic lead. The movie, directed by Mexico's Alfonso Arau, is actually a remake of a 1942 Italian film and has a dreamy, European feel. Keanu plays Paul Sutton, a shell-shocked soldier returning home to civilian life in 1945 to discover that the wife he hastily married hasn't even read his hundreds of letters. Resuming his job as a chocolate salesman, he catches a train and begins talking to a soulful woman (played by Spanish newcomer Aitana Sanchez-Gijon) who reveals that she has been made pregnant by a college professor and fears her Mexican-American father will kill her for dishonoring the family. Gentlemanly Keanu offers to pretend to be her husband temporarily so that she can return home. But her vineyard-owner father is furious that his daughter has married a lowly traveling salesman, although the rest of the family, including her grandfather (Anthony Quinn), is more welcoming. Before long, though, Sutton realizes he's falling in love.

Playing a sensitive, Gary Cooper type was a challenge, but one Keanu was eager to accept. "I was shooting *Speed* when I met Alfonso and I was attracted by the idea of doing a romance because it was so different. After *Speed* I wanted to work on the heart and emotions. Believe me, falling out of a car has got nothing on falling in love!" To prepare for the role, he watched all of Cooper's films and during filming insisted on staying in character between scenes.

"It was a tough test for him," agrees Arau. "He was stressed and insecure about it and sometimes I had to get him to lighten up—I had to tell him, 'be more like a woman, not a man.'" But the director was impressed by the actor's determination. "Keanu is like a monk," he says. "He is devoted to his craft, and has an innocence of spirit that this particular character needed."

By all accounts, Keanu hit it off with veteran actor Anthony Quinn, who first shot to fame in *Zorba the Greek* more than thirty years earlier. "I found an old Hollywood glamour magazine on the set and Anthony would go, 'I knew her and her and her,'" says Keanu with a chuckle. "I felt I was in the presence of a legend." And the two joked and chatted at the L.A. premiere of *A Walk in the Clouds*, also attended by Keanu's sparring partner in *Speed*, Dennis Hopper, and by Geena Davis, Diane Keaton, and James Coburn.

However, yet again the critics poured scorn on the actor's performance. One reviewer gave him a "worst kiss of the year award" for "a peck on the cheek that wouldn't frighten his auntie." A teen magazine claimed that Arau tried to get him to improve his sloppy kissing technique by watching Kevin Costner videos. "Where do they get that stuff?" he sighs. Another critic scoffed, "Poor Reeves, God bless him, looks non-plussed throughout. His performance doesn't lack range, though—it runs the gamut from mild perplexity to total bafflement." But this time, despite such sniping, Keanu had the last laugh, with the film grossing a respectable $50 million in America alone.

Yet no star, however big, is immune from box-office failure. And that's as true for Keanu Reeves as it is for Tom Cruise, Julia Roberts, Brad Pitt, or Johnny Depp. But as 1996 dawned, Keanu was as busy as ever, with at three least films in the pipeline.

The first, *Feeling Minnesota*, stared Keanu and Cameron Diaz (who shot to fame in *The Mask*) as lovers on the run; the twist is that she just happens to be married to his brother.

Keanu and Anthony Quinn in A Walk in the Clouds

The film came from Danny De Vito's Jersey Films, a company with a knack for coming up with offbeat hits, such as *Pulp Fiction* and *Get Shorty*. A film noir–style black comedy, it also featured cameos from comic Dan Aykroyd and grunge queen Courtney Love, widow of Nirvana's tragic frontman Kurt Cobain.

Another big-budget movie, *Chain Reaction* (directed by Andrew Davis, best known for making *The Fugitive*) was billed by it's studio, Fox, as a "nonstop thriller." Also starring Morgan Freeman, the movie concerned a streetwise lab technician (Keanu) on the run after being framed for murder.

Several years after *Speed*, Keanu is as big a star as ever. Almost any store selling movie-related paraphernalia boasts a wall of Keanu postcards, photographs, and posters. What's more, a California university set up a course to study his films. His popularity is also reflected in the number of Keanu pages on the Internet. Fans all over the world have set up their own web sites devoted to the object of their affection, many with jokey names like Temple Keanu or the Dude Da Lama. There is even a tongue-in-cheek religious order, The Society of Keanu Consciousness, whose guiding principle is to be excellent to each other.

Of course, nothing is certain in the fickle world of the movies. But whatever happens, it seems likely that Keanu Reeves will be around for a long time.

FILMOGRAPHY

The year refers to the first release date of the film.

1986   *Youngblood*
1986   *River's Edge*
1988   *The Night Before*
1988   *Prince of Pennsylvania*
1988   *Permanent Record*
1988   *Dangerous Liaisons*
1989   *Bill & Ted's Excellent Adventure*
1989   *Parenthood*
1990   *I Love You to Death*
1990   *Aunt Julia and the Scriptwriter (aka Tune in Tomorrow)*
1991   *Point Break*
1991   *My Own Private Idaho*
1991   *Bill & Ted's Bogus Journey*
1992   *Bram Stoker's Dracula*
1993   *Much Ado About Nothing*
1993   *Little Buddha*
1994   *Speed*
1994   *Even Cowgirls Get the Blues*
1995   *A Walk in the Clouds*
1995   *Johnny Mnemonic*
1996   *Feeling Minnesota*
1996   *Chain Reaction*
1997   *The Last Time I Committed Suicide*
1997   *Devil's Advocate*

INDEX

47

INDEX